BEGINNING EXPERIENCES IN ARCHITECTURE

BEGINNING EXPERIENCES IN ARCHITECTURE

A Guide for the Elementary School Teacher

George E. Trogler

Photographs by Marjorie Pickens

VNR **VAN NOSTRAND REINHOLD COMPANY**
NEW YORK   CINCINNATI   TORONTO   LONDON   MELBOURNE

Van Nostrand Reinhold Company Regional Offices:
New York   Cincinnati   Chicago   Millbrae   Dallas

Van Nostrand Reinhold Company International Offices:
London   Toronto   Melbourne

All photographs by Marjorie Pickens except where otherwise
indicated
Designed by Beverly T. Lavick and Jean Callan King
Printed by Halliday Lithograph Corporation
Bound by Publishers Book Bindery, Inc.

Published by Van Nostrand Reinhold Company
450 West 33rd Street, New York, N.Y. 10001

Published simultaneously in Canada by
Van Nostrand Reinhold Company Ltd.

16   15   14   13   12   11   10   9   8   7   6   5   4   3   2   1

ACKNOWLEDGMENTS

Numerous people and organizations have inspired, assisted, and encouraged this project. I would like to thank the following:

The faculty, parents, children, and staff of the Nicholas Murray Butler School #23, Elizabeth, New Jersey. Especially Edith Thompson, principal, and Ruth Bressler and her first- and second-grade class of 1969-70. Without their co-operation this would never have happened.

The Board of Education and Central Administration, Elizabeth, New Jersey. John E. Dwyer, Superintendent; Rocco J. Colelli, Assistant to the Superintendent; and Marion Quin Dix, Director of Art Education.

The New Jersey State Department of Education; The United States Office of Education; Western Pennsylvania Conservancy.

Benoist, Goldberg, and Shapiro, AIA; Ronald Silber.

Mary Mooty, Ivan Johnson, and Julia Schwartz of Florida State University.

Rowena Reed Kostellow and Charles M. Robertson of Pratt Institute.

Nancy Newman and Barbara Klinger of Van Nostrand Reinhold Company.

TO ELLA M. McGREGOR

CONTENTS

INTRODUCTION

As I survey the landscapes of suburbia I am confronted by a sameness. The thousands of split-level look-alikes are only one example of how accepting and uncritical the affluent public has become when selecting architecture for domestic needs. In addition, the "Colonial" adaptations and "brick-walled monsters" featured as model houses and apartments in the Sunday newspapers reflect an economy where the latest electrical appliance or kitchen convenience is expected to sell a house before its architectural merit. If the public is accepting of mediocre building and continues to patronize the builder who profits from unimaginative work, the architect can be expected to continue to design dull, uninteresting buildings.

Now more than ever, architectural experiences should play a vital role in the schools. For too long architecture has been neglected and seldom approached in the elementary school. It seems essential and valuable for young children to have experiences that capture the dynamics of space and architecture. As adults these children will be called upon to make decisions that affect the appearance of their communities. If elements and principles of art are considered in isolation from the everyday environment and the active daily lives of children, they can easily be forgotten and overlooked as insignificant. Terms like line, plane, volume, space, color, and texture should not be left in the art room. If related to everyday living, these principles and elements may begin to have

Experiences that allow children to see the dynamics of forms and planes in space result in a more imaginative approach to architecture.

9

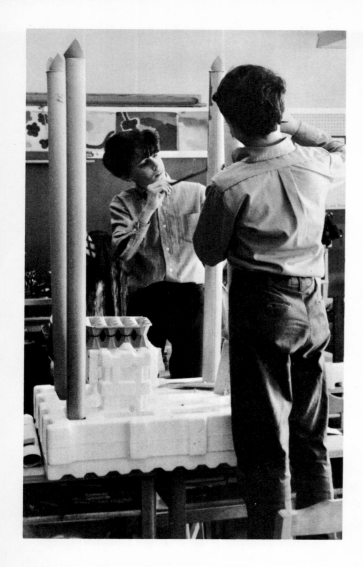

When building models and drawing architectural pictures, terms like line, plane and volume are related to everyday life and become more relevant.

Lauren

Randy

The principles and elements of art are more easily remembered as children incorpo-rate them into models. An "A" frame house may emphasize linear structure; other models may stress elements like mass.

a relevance and therefore may begin to capture a position of importance in the learning process.

In teaching art or architecture to children, an atmosphere for discovery and experimentation should be encouraged by the teacher's energy and enthusiasm. There will be no way to know if a "Le Corbusier" or a "Frank Lloyd Wright" might be among the members of the class. There will be only the challenge to offer the most that can possibly be offered for whatever benefits the children in the class may receive. Perhaps no architectural genius will emerge, but instead half a dozen or more citizens who care and are concerned about architecture and their environment. This should be reward enough. The impact of these students on their environment can be equally vital in establishing a pattern for future generations.

A primary objective for the teacher should be to encourage experiences that will increase a student's perception of architecture and develop his ability to organize and manipulate art materials. Some projects inevitably stretch the imagination and achieve more highly speculative results than others. Problems in experiencing space, structure, and form are fundamental and should be challenging. Although a child's own house seems suitable as the most natural point of ref-

One goal is to increase a student's perception and his ability to manipulate all kinds of art materials.

erence because it is a building to which children can relate most easily through past association, a stereotyped picture of a square house with peaked roof and "lollipop" trees is an image that is not always easy to erase from the mind. Using an approach based on past association is only a beginning and is limited in scope. Drawing a picture of their own homes does help children become more aware of materials used in construction and more aware of the placement of doors, windows, and architectural detail. However, this exercise provides little opportunity for inventive design.

It is more productive to see what a young mind might create with the motivation, opportunity, and materials to invent more exciting forms. To do this, it is essential to provide ideas that cause children to forget the many poor architectural examples they have seen and to continually think beyond those examples. Not only are children open to suggestion and quick to try new experiences but they also have an intuitive sense of balance and a desire for organization in their designs. Although young children need not be concerned about practical structures and they are content with the joy and fascination of building

Most children seem to have an intuitive sense of design and a desire for balance and organization in their work.

temporary models, the imaginative solutions they devise for architectural problems can provide ideas for future architectural adaptations by experts.

Because children are freed of building codes, costs, and clients, their designs are more likely to be fresh and imaginative. They should not be limited by the usual standards. Some projects will have a visual impact that borders on the fringe of fantasy, while others will be closely related to sculpture. Let children imagine and design a housing unit on another planet or under the water's surface, and see what happens.

An excellent way of challenging unknowing minds to make creative decisions is to show children architecture that incorporates modern technology and uses materials in forms and structures that are new and different. For example, slides and pictures of Frank Lloyd Wright's "Fallingwater" house, with its use of concrete in cantilevered construction, can inspire children to create "Dream Houses" never before imagined. Pictures of Habitat in Montreal, Canada, can be the basis for many projects utilizing the principle of stacking modules.

Although there are numerous approaches to

Pictures of modern structures and materials inspire children in their own creative work. Cantilevered construction is shown by Frank Lloyd Wright's "Fallingwater" house. (Photograph at left by Michael Fedison. Courtesy of Western Pennsylvania Conservancy.) Habitat (below) shows the principle of stacking modules. (Photograph by the author.)

architecture, this book is based on my firsthand experiences in relating architectural concepts to children within the framework of a one-period-per-week art program in a city elementary school encompassing kindergarten to sixth grade. The pictures of children working were taken during the regular art periods and serve to reflect an interest that often stretched the minimum forty-five-minute class to sixty minutes or longer. The study of architecture at this early age level was not intended to become separate from the art program. It was only one portion of the total curriculum.

Architecture is interrelated with other subjects. A social studies course evoked interest in making a model of an American Indian home.

the design possibilities of skyscrapers and of molded and poured architectural shells. There was a constant interaction between the other subjects the children studied and their work in the art program. Model-building, for example, gave children the opportunity to apply their knowledge of geometry and arithmetic and stimulated new interest in those subjects.

Accurate measuring for model-making stimulated a new desire for mathematical knowledge.

The whole school shared in the excitement and opportunities provided by the incorporation of architecture into the curriculum. A concentrated study of architecture in the home and community started with one first grade and continued during the second grade. Third graders became interested in the architecture of the American Indian as they learned about that culture in their social studies unit. Other individual and group interests were accommodated as they arose. One fifth-grade class worked for about a month discovering

Children began to talk about their work and were anxious to increase their vocabularies in order to communicate.

The study of architectural concepts also creates new avenues of investigation. Students learn, for instance, that interior and exterior scenes of buildings were often used by Renaissance painters to reveal social, economic, and cultural conditions, and that such paintings can be a source of historical information.

Clearly, the idea of architecture, although most closely related to art in concept and study, is not limited to designing. In considering career opportunities, a look at the highly skilled and specialized services offered by large architectural firms shows occupational possibilities which overlap many other vocations, such as city planner and developer, landscape architect, model-maker, renderer, draftsman, architectural historian and critic.

A valuable addition to the curriculum, the classes in art and architecture that I taught also had some unexpected side benefits in the areas of communication and co-operation. As first graders finished their pictures or projects, they were eager to tell about them. Their one-line descriptions became two-line descriptions; then paragraphs and stories developed. It seemed to take forever for me to write down what thirty-two children wanted to say, and yet the children were talking only about their art work.

The solution to this secretarial problem emerged when some fifth graders volunteered their help. With pad and pencil, five fifth-grade secretaries reported for duty. It was explained that someone else would have to read their writing and therefore it was essential to write or print legibly. Penmanship and spelling have never been better. Other fifth graders asked to take turns. Some were able to encourage the first graders who were too shy to talk to adults.

Once written, the children's stories were pasted onto the pictures or models they had made or below Polaroid photographs taken during the art period. Folders containing the stories and pictures of recent projects were kept in the classroom library and could be taken out overnight by the students, who enjoyed bringing home this crystallization of their experiences. And, as the children's vocabularies grew, they were able to share more and more of their classroom experiences with their parents.

The classroom experiences were varied. In some instances, there were formal, structured beginnings. In other cases, lessons focused on ar-

Taking home portfolios of their work enabled children to share their classroom experiences with their parents.

chitecture according to the inspiration provided by the art materials at hand. Some projects were approached more than once. This was especially true with problems involving concepts and principles that were complex and, as you will discover, suggestive of a variety of solutions. Consequently, there was no reason for a chronological list of activities to be made, although one lesson could become the foundation for another.

For my own purposes, I outlined a total program based on individual and classroom characteristics, as well as on the materials and physical facilities offered by the school. Because no two schools are the same in terms of these considerations I present a composite of my experiences for individual interpretation and application. It should be remembered that, as children and teachers differ in background and ability, individual and unique approaches necessitate experimentation.

If young children were able to comprehend basic architectural concepts by participating in the program described here, adults with similar inexperience should have no trouble understanding and conducting the suggested explorations. With a minimum of preliminary investigation, and using this book as a guide, teachers and parents will be able to open up the world of architecture to children. The only prerequisite is an ability to be open to new experiences and receptive to new architectural solutions. Although this book is intended for use by the amateur, the experiences related in it might also prove interesting for those with architectural knowledge.

MATERIALS

When Frank Lloyd Wright was young, his mother gave him a set of building blocks. Later in life, he still remembered the experiences he had using them and implied that they had been helpful in his architecture.

Using blocks to develop manipulatory skills is important in early childhood education. Try giving your students building blocks with the direction, "Build the tallest building you can," and watch what happens. I find blocks are a natural beginning and should be in every classroom. Too often blocks are seen in the kindergarten and then forgotten.

Elementary school children enjoy using blocks with little if any direction from the teacher. They will see how many ways they can find to construct tall buildings. They can be directed to see how high they can build structures using the least number of blocks and to consider the open spaces created by their structures to see if the spaces form patterns as interesting as the three-dimensional volumes.

Besides regular wooden blocks, giant foam blocks are also available. If they fall down, towering structures of foam will crash quietly without disturbing the rest of the class. Scraps of wood from lumberyards and from buildings under construction make suitable building blocks if the pieces are clean and smooth. They need not be painted, as children can visualize color schemes

Manipulatory devices, foam blocks, and sand are all vital materials for learning. Sand is especially favored by children.

in their imaginations. Materials get children involved in learning because they are able to make discoveries for themselves. Building blocks are only one beginning. There are additional manipulatory devices which stack or slot and fit together. Their educational validity should not be overlooked just because they also function as playthings which children enjoy using. Some of these devices are listed under Supplementary Materials and should be used as budgets allow.

Another basic material is sand. Anyone who has built a castle in the sand knows of the excitement it offers in designing. I have found that children especially like to push and model it with their hands. Paper and plastic forms can be used for making molds if the sand is moistened with water. A sandbox might suggest a seashore, another planet, a desert, a Japanese garden, or the perfect place to build a castle depending on the mood of a child or the directions of a perceptive teacher. If a commercially manufactured sandbox is not available, a strong but shallow cardboard box might be used to hold the sand. Individual sandboxes, made by filling metal or plastic containers (such as garbage-can lids) with several inches of sand, can be taken outside, where the children are free to experiment with a minimum of cleaning up afterward.

Materials that are easily available and inexpensive offer endless possibilities for model-making experiences. Tin cans can be stacked; newspapers can be rolled into structural supports; even discarded film spools can become a building material.

The opportunity to select from a variety of materials provides impetus for limitless imaginative and inventive solutions to architectural projects. School supplies can be combined with materials assembled by the children, who will find use for many items often thrown away at home. Materials that are easily available and inexpensive offer endless combinations for model-making. A basic list would include: wood, sand, cardboard boxes, flat cardboard, tubes, foamed plastic, packaging containers, egg crates, vegetable baskets, meat trays, nylon stockings, sugar cubes, soda straws, toothpicks, metal screens, newspaper, papier-mâché, Pariscraft, string, balloons, and a variety of papers. Cardboard cut from boxes makes adequate bases for most projects.

As children bring in "throwaways" from home large plastic bags or cardboard boxes can be used for temporary storage. If storage rooms are not available, a corner in the classroom can be organized to hold these supplies.

Knowing and understanding the characteristics of model-making materials is important for both teacher and students. Some projects warrant stiff, rigid materials, while others suggest more pliable substances. The characteristics of the model-making materials may not always parallel the characteristics of the architectural materials. Projects illustrating the principles of molded structures, for instance, may rely on flexible paper to capture the curves of a molded form that would be executed in concrete.

Knowing the characteristics of model-building materials is important. Cardboard is good for showing angular planes; styrofoam has a massive look.

Rigid pieces of cardboard can be glued together for models of frame structures actually built of steel; flexible paper is more suitable for curved forms like those built of poured concrete.

31

When I approach a concept for the first time, I look for suitable materials. Then I consider the objectives of the experience. If children are to construct tall buildings using the principle of stacking, the most direct solution is to use preformed units that are rigid enough to support each other. Geometrically shaped blocks of wood or foam have already been mentioned. In addition, paper cups, boxes, packaging containers, cans, and sugar cubes all could be used without an adhesive. It usually requires more time for children to create their own units for stacking. Paper or thin cardboard is easily folded or rolled, and can be glued or stapled.

One of the simplest modules to make for stacking is a prism based on the equilateral triangle. A long strip of paper is folded horizontally into quarters, forming four equal segments. With the folded paper reopened, the two end segments are overlapped and glued together to form the prism. Other suitable modules can be constructed by folding or rolling rectangular strips of paper, oak tag, or cardboard into cubes, rectangles, and cylinders. These individual units can be stacked and grouped in colorful and imaginative ways. Surfaces can be left plain or given additional embel-

(Above) Arches, domes, and other curved forms require pliable materials like plastic reeds.

(Left) Styrofoam cups offer preformed units suitable for stacking into tall buildings.

lishment. The building-block units of Habitat offer inspiration for an endless variety of asymmetrical, modular arrangements. The openness of Habitat's design is in definite contrast to most apartment buildings constructed with a central lobby and miles of closed corridors. Although Habitat was built recently, its appearance is reminiscent of the pueblos found in the Southwestern United States.

Structures based on continuous arches or curved movements in space require model-making materials that can be bent or twisted. I found paper strips, plastic reeds, and long strips of wood ideal for young children. Older children were able to bend wire. Papier-mâché permits children of all ages to fashion both domes and curved shells. Preformed domes can be discovered in some packaging containers or by inverting bowls. A trip to a supermarket can help train the eye to see packaging containers of suitable shapes.

Discarded bed sheets, scraps of fabric, nylon stockings, and plastic are flexible and serve to cover linear skeletons and space frames as examples of soft-skin architecture. Additional materials used for model-making and for experiencing space are mentioned in Chapter 3.

The students should know the characteristics of the architectural materials used in structures as well as the characteristics of the model-making materials they use. The best way to accomplish this is to allow the students to actually experience the weight and texture of materials like brick, stone, and wood (and, if possible, the modern synthetic materials like foamed plastics, which are strong but lightweight). If children run their fingers over the surfaces of these materials they can experience qualities of hardness, roughness, coldness, and warmth. As they investigate more fully by handling these materials in the classroom, they can get some idea of size, shape, and weight. They can be asked to look outside the classroom for buildings of similar materials. By looking at rooftops, walls, and other details, children can become aware of additional characteristics in these materials. Walls of brick might reveal varied stacking and grouping possibilities. An arrange-

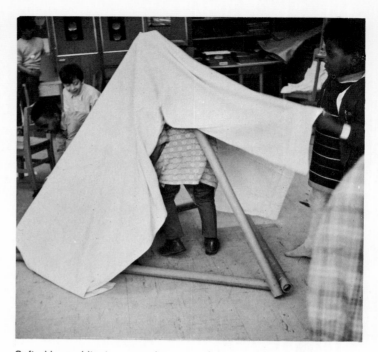

Soft-skin architecture can be created by covering linear skeletons with bed sheets or other fabric.

By handling stones and bricks in the classroom, children experience such qualities as the weight and texture of architectural materials.

ment of wooden shingles might be seen as a visual pattern stressing rhythm. The surfaces of stones may be seen differently as they are cut and polished.

These visual and tactile perceptions are part of a learning process in which one discovery leads to another. Perceptions evolve and change as discoveries are made and new information is added. Because they are constantly in the process of adding new information and therefore changing former perceptions, visual and tactile perceptions can be considered "in-process perceptions." If creative learning and discovery are to occur, these kinesthetic and sensitizing experiences of handling and observation are essential.

The opportunities for these experiences are provided in the classroom by making available samples of architectural materials and outside the classroom by taking the children on exploratory trips, which are discussed further in Chapter 4. Seeing and relating real examples of architectural materials in the community outside the classroom helps children to develop a total perception.

From time to time, the teacher might ask children to make a picture of what they have built or of an experience they have had. Paper and other drawing materials such as felt-tip markers, crayons, chalks, paints, or pencils should be available. I have found that crayon and chalk interpretations are quite different from those done

After building a structure (above), a child may draw his experience (opposite page). A variety of drawing materials should be provided, as an interpretation done in crayon will differ from one done in paint.

in paint. The latter seems more difficult for most children to manipulate, and its use as a drawing material should be considered accordingly.

Motivations are often as important as the materials provided. The major need is to encourage experiences that will increase a student's desire to investigate and solve architectural problems by handling art materials. Suggestions for motivating students are given throughout the book. The classroom itself should be set up to facilitate motivation as well as provide a place to work.

Adequate work space fosters creativity.

2
CLASSROOM FACILITIES AND ORGANIZATION

Children need space to work. From a practical point of view, the nature of architectural investigations requires space. A towering skyscraper without glue will undoubtedly fall and there should be enough room for it to tumble without hitting the work of others, if at all possible. Adequate space is also important in fostering creativity. In an art program such as this, an atmosphere conducive to discovery and experimentation needs to be encouraged from the beginning. To set the stage, classroom furniture can be pushed together to form large tables and also provide empty areas for working on the floor. An empty floor allows designing freedom not permitted by a desk top, and children should be able to select where they prefer working.

Working outside in pleasant weather extends the classroom. Inside, all available space is utilized, including the blackboard, which is covered with paper for drawing murals.

Since learning does not occur in a vacuum and motivation will play an important part in approaching each principle or concept that is to be investigated, the classroom should have facilities for a large variety of motivational aids. My own multimedia/multi-sensory approach to teaching requires every inch of space in the art room or classroom to be utilized. The blackboard is used for making class murals; rolls of paper are stretched across a wall to provide drawing space. Pictures from books and magazines, and art reproductions, are continuously displayed on bulletin boards or on panels of Homosote. (Besides

Equipment for projecting 35mm slides and for projecting opaque pictures are also kept accessible for ready use.

(Left) Sketching trips outside the classroom relate learning to actuality. (Above) Three-dimensional models are used to point out linear movement, while art reproductions, such as this Cubist interpretation of juxtaposed planes, are used to motivate learning.

serving to illustrate principles of structure and space, art reproductions show that buildings have been a source of subject matter for many artists — Utrillo, Monet, and Canaletto, for example — for hundreds of years and thus add an incentive for the students to make sketching trips in the neighborhood.) Three-dimensional models and manipulatory materials are kept close at hand.

Looking at three-dimensional models, slides and pictures increases children's perception of architecture.

In the Introduction, I mentioned the impact that slides and pictures of Wright's "Fallingwater" had on the children's work. The overhead projector is an equally valuable visual aid, projecting small shapes so that they are large enough for everyone in a classroom to see. To increase visual perception, I may project, one at a time, simple geometric shapes cut from construction paper. Some of these shapes have holes cut from their centers or pieces cut from their sides. After each shape is shown, the child is to draw it from memory. After about ten shapes are projected and drawn, the child is to cut them out and then fold them or fasten them together in order to form a standing, playground sculpture. He may combine them in any way he wishes and color the surfaces as he desires.

Construction-paper shapes can be projected to show, in silhouette, many varieties of building shapes. I usually start with a square and demonstrate how the slant, curve, or peak of a roof can alter the visual impression of the original shape. By adding squares, triangles, and rectangles onto the original square, larger and more varied shapes can be developed. Domes and free-form shapes can also be shown.

Silhouettes of colored cellophanes and plastics arranged on a sheet of clear plastic provide additional visual impact as the transparent colors are projected. Although they are more expensive than paper, I recommend Bourges Cutocolor and Cutotapes (colored plastics with adhesive backings) for making a series of overlays on clear plastic. Separate shapes on separate overlays can be built up to the final form layer by layer. These overlays are especially helpful in showing the shapes and placement of doors and windows. The relationship and importance of landscaping to architecture can be seen through a series of

side, and top views of the same model. Children are then able to make the relationships more easily.

Children can experiment with construction paper and project their own ideas for the class. Using sheets of heavy acetate, the student can arrange his work at his seat and then carry it when finished to the overhead projector.

Pictures from magazines can be transferred to Mylar plastic and projected. The plastic, which is coated with an adhesive, sticks to the ink-base print. After the picture has been soaked for a period of time in water, the paper content can be rubbed off, leaving only colored ink on the plastic, and the back of the transparency can be coated with clear acrylic paint or laminated with another sheet of plastic to protect it.

Besides the overhead projector and the slide projector other equipment may be called into use for special occasions, such as showing motion pictures about art or architecture. If the classroom is small, the class might adjourn to the school auditorium for these showings and also for projects that require more room than the classroom allows. If the weather is pleasant the class can be conducted outside in the school yard.

Facilities should also be provided for the dis-

overlays using bushes, trees, shrubs, flowers, roads, and walks placed on top of the layer showing a house. By projecting the use and placement of a "groundline" the teacher can help beginners in organizing two-dimensional compositions.

The overhead projector can also be used to relate two-dimensional graphic symbols to three-dimensional models. A simple three-dimensional model of a building with a removable roof can be compared with graphic overlays showing front, play and recognition of finished projects. Displaying accomplishments is important and can be used as part of continued motivation. I have given older children the opportunity to show their three-dimensional models in the classrooms of the younger children. Unfinished work should also have a designated place for safekeeping, such as a locker or a cabinet. As with materials, if no outside space is available, an area of the classroom can be organized for the purpose.

In addition to visual aids, classroom organization should take into account other stimuli. Reading Carl Sandburg's poem "Skyscraper" to the class might suggest to the children that they write about buildings they know as well as interpreting them graphically. Andreas Feininger's book *Form in Nature and Life** can be used to present the idea that animal homes and structures in nature serve as a constant source of inspiration. The intricate weaving of a bird's nest and the honeycomb of a beehive suggest inventiveness with materials as well as structural adaptations for building. The various structures of ferns, leaves, and spider webs are not only visually appealing but equally suitable for construction principles. Supplying motivation is a very important part of making the program succeed.

*See Bibliography.

Other visual stimuli, such as the overhead projector (opposite page) and forms from nature (wasp's nest above), provoke interest in perspective and structure.

Exploring the concept of space through physical participation is the best way for many children to understand it. Later, they translate these experiences into drawings.

3
THE PROGRAM

Part I: Space

EXPERIENCING SPACE

Any number of strategies can be employed in introducing and developing a principle or a concept. Exploring architectural concepts through physical participation in exercises that involve the whole body is the way many children understand and remember learning best. The concept of space especially should be investigated through the kinesthetic sense. Space cannot be measured and understood in terms of two dimensions but must be estimated and experienced in three-dimensional relationships. Explorations that

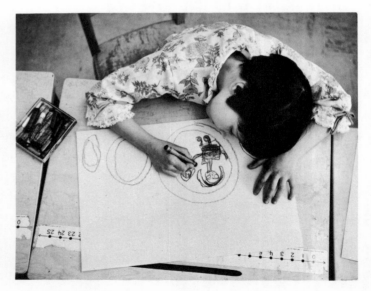

Drawings reflect children's involvement in experiencing space. Walking through a pipe was remembered from a trip. Other explorations can include weaving around cardboard walls.

require crawling into cardboard boxes, walking under arches, or weaving in and around rolls of corrugated cardboard set up to suggest the walls of a building are realistic examples of how students can and do experience space.

Imaginative playground sculpture presents similar opportunities for children to experience space kinesthetically, calling upon them to crawl and stretch as they climb or jump from one place to another. The scale is one to which they feel a part and can relate because it is proportionate to their own size. A house or an apartment building is immense and overwhelming, and a small box or a few pieces of paper are too small. The empty space of a large cardboard box, however, always seems to provide an invitation for children to "play house." To them, the box can seem like a small apartment or a place for privacy. They can

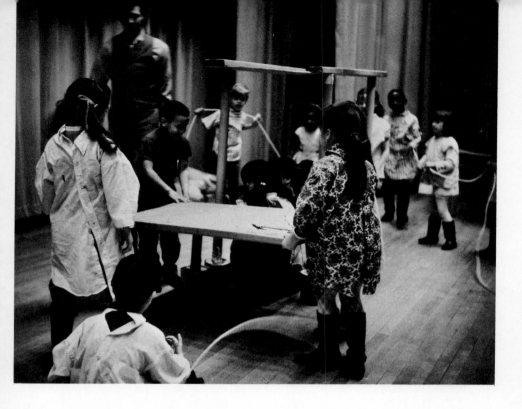

Using cardboard tubes and cut-up boxes, children build their own shelter. They also explore openings cut out of corrugated walls.

pretend that this space belongs to them because it is in proportion to their own size. For children the activities may seem more like play than problems in design, but when introduced by a perceptive teacher these experiences may pave the way for future architectural development.

The importance of having children participate in these experiences is that it involves them in a total motivation and leads to making many discoveries. When introducing a study of structural shells that are molded or poured, I ask children to place the palms of their hands flat on a desk top and to watch what happens as they slowly push upward with their fingertips. They should be able to see that space is defined as their fingers push their hands upward. The shell of the hand, they discover, creates an interior cavity that can be changed as their fingers slowly move up and down as well as in and out.

As the wrist and arm are included in this discovery of space, each child can be encouraged to bend and move his entire body in a dance called "Capturing Space," with the gestures symbolizing free-form architectural shapes for the future. Students can incorporate desks and tables as they need support in taking new positions. Or

they might group themselves in forms representative of space shells. Stopping for gesture drawing will create a link to architectural form. If children are to think abstractly, in terms other than the rigid, stereotyped house with pokey windows, they must discover the dynamics of the dimensions of space.

Playful activity is meaningful in discovering the dynamic aspects of space.

ORGANIZING SPACE

Once children have experienced space, they can begin to think in terms of organizing it. I like to introduce children to the idea of organizing space by having them all hold onto a long rope and form straight and curved lines. As the open areas in the classroom or on the playground are enclosed by the rope, shapes are defined. When the rope is then dropped to the floor, the straight and curved lines that were formed make a linear pattern similar to a floor plan and show how the space was organized. Large rolls of corrugated cardboard can be set up along the rope pattern to represent free-standing walls and show how the space is shaped in three dimensions by adding upright

planes. In this way, children are also able to establish the connection between the interior space (defined first by the rope outline and then by the cardboard) and the exterior form created in space by the cardboard walls.

It might seem that the simplest way to approach the subject of organizing space is by introducing floor plans, which to the adult mind are two-dimensional representations from an aerial view of the way space is defined and arranged in three dimensions. However, I have found that translating three-dimensional objects into two-dimensional symbols is difficult for children. In addition, I found that most floor plans that appear in magazines and in the real-estate sections of city newspapers represent box-type rooms placed within

larger boxes, with walls that fence in space instead of organizing it imaginatively. These examples restrict children from being creative in their own attempts at designing.

I did find that the concept of aerial perspective interested children in exploring the organization of space. Children like to pretend and will readily accept the idea of an imaginary airplane ride. If you ask children to pretend that all the roofs have been taken off the buildings in the community, they will be eager to "board" their airplane to get a better look. As they are flying high in the sky, a visual picture can be painted in words of what the children can see if they look *straight down* over the landscape. The children can then be asked to show, with paper and pencil or crayons, what they have visualized. A picture drawn of their own house or school, or even an imaginary building, will reveal if the concept of aerial perspective is clear. Symbols for doors and windows can be devised as they are needed. It is not necessary to present these symbols to children who have not grasped the concept of aerial perspective and are still drawing elevations.

Experimenting further, children can cut out strips of paper and arrange them on the desk top,

A long, thin rectangle of paper is folded and made to stand to define space. After this paper sculpture experience, a second grader drew this imaginative floor plan.

Sugar cubes are used for beginning experiences in organizing space. Three-dimensional models introduce the concept of planes in space; a simple fold breaks the otherwise flat surface of a piece of cardboard.

or on a cardboard base, to suggest arrangements of lines that define space on a flat surface without completely fencing it in. Open spaces can represent windows and walls of glass. A breakup and arrangement of space becomes the primary concern in these floor-plan designs, which can be either functional or non-functional.

Building and examining three-dimensional models with vertical, curved, and inclined planes goes even further in helping children read floor plans and understand space. The flat, two-dimensional surface of a floor plan can serve as the base on which to erect these planes.

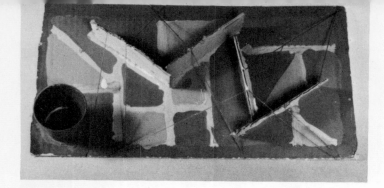

(Left) Non-functional breakup of space directs the eye from one area to another. Upright pieces of cardboard partition the space; string adds a linear element. (Below) Corrugated cardboard creates curved walls. (Opposite page) Additional levels make the design more complicated.

PLANES IN SPACE

Instead of arranging strips of paper on a flat surface, children can begin to define space with planes that stand perpendicular to the flat surface. Using a sheet of cardboard as a base, upright walls and partitions of cardboard can be placed and glued in dynamic patterns that open up space. Corrugated cardboard might be incorporated in creating walls that curve. String running from one point to another adds a linear element that can further capture space when the lines are grouped together or can offer unity to a design when the lines are used singly to lead the eye from one solid plane to another.

Models built on several levels with inclined planes as ramps or stairs make the design rela-

As horizontal and slanted roofs are added to models, children begin to see that planes create movements in space. Folds of a paper sculpture create a faceted wall. Cardboard can be arranged so that all the planes radiate from one point.

tionships more complicated. Spirals cut from paper create continuous movements in space. In all designing, it is necessary to remember that the open spaces should be as important as the structural members in creating cavities for living. Young designers should approach architecture as an exercise in spatial geometry and they can find inspiration for this in the work of Frank Lloyd Wright. The fact that children are most familiar with boxlike rooms should also be considered. It may take time for them to learn that if a roof is added to a model it need not conform to the shape of the floor space. Peaked, slanted, flat, domed, and vaulted roofs offer endless varieties.

As three-dimensional models are built and horizontal or peaked roofs are added to the upright partitions or inclined ramps and spirals are included, the children can see that the various planes create different movements in space. An upright plane leads the eye in a vertical direction, while an inclined ramp leads the eye in a diagonal direction.

The slowly curving ramp of New York's Guggenheim Museum is an adventure in three dimensions.

The vertical thrust of a Brancusi sculpture can be related to the visual movement created by a tall building. Children learn about this movement by pretending to be vertical columns.

LINEAR MOVEMENT IN SPACE

Architecture is concerned with movements in space. In crowded cities the only way to build is up, and the vertical movement of the modern skyscraper has become a visible and dramatic part of almost every large city. In the suburbs, the ranch-style home provides a contrast, with its long, low, horizontal movement.

Children can experience such movements in space by imitating them. Ask children to position themselves as tall, stiff buildings by standing erect and still. Ask children to bend and move their bodies to suggest the spiral ramp in the Guggenheim Museum. They can stretch and curve their arms toward the sky as a Gothic arch or join hands as a group and form a dome. As they hold hands and form a circular movement or create a serpentine wall you can begin to create an interest in the way different shapes and planes suggest different movements.

This unification of planes and their movements becomes apparent in the actual building of structures. Though at this point children need not be concerned with specific structures, the discovery that any construction in space shows a basic

65

Preformed units such as foam blocks and wooden rectangles are collected for stacking modules to create simple horizontal or vertical movements. Paper strips are folded into triangular units to assemble another structure.

movement is significant. Stacking or grouping various materials and preformed units gives children the opportunity to make their own constructions illustrating simple vertical or horizontal movements. Building blocks, boxes, sugar cubes, or other manipulative devices allow for both symmetrical and asymmetrical designs. Educational toys are available commercially and will demonstrate the possibilities of joining preformed modules.

Young children prefer working with preformed units, which allow various groupings and arrangements. Towers and skyscrapers are popular projects concerned with balance and vertical movement.

While young children enjoy using preformed units, older children can be expected to assemble elaborate towers and skyscrapers from cardboard. Small squares and rectangles of cardboard are among the best materials to use. They can be cut on the paper cutter before class and, once distributed, they can be glued together in endless combinations that might suggest a complex house of cards. Because balance is a problem while the glue is drying, small units can be assembled first and stacked together after the glue has hardened.

The juxtaposition of various planes and their movements in space is an important consideration in emphasizing imaginative designs. Dominant, sub-dominant, and subordinate movements interlock and overlap each other to provide much more dynamic structures than the boxlike rooms that most people are used to.

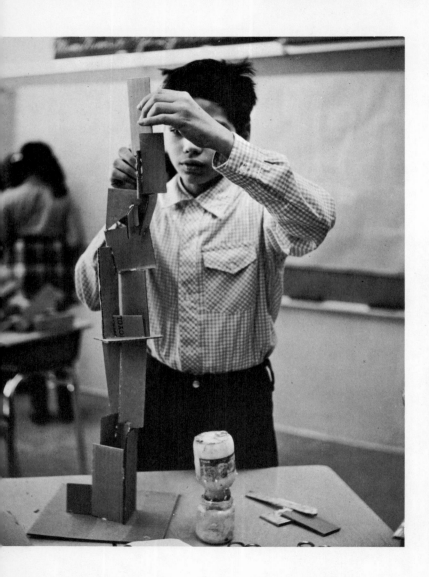

A juxtaposition and balance of shapes and forms is emphasized in architectural prototypes that I refer to as "Big Box Buildings." Before I bring any boxes to class, I cut off at least one side to keep the boxes from being used only as cubes. In arranging these boxes, children combine them with flat sheets of cardboard and even with classroom furniture to create an interaction of planes. Some of these imaginative designs have porches

Older children are more apt to build complex towers from small pieces of cardboard.

"Big Box Buildings" show an interaction of planes and allow children to investigate how the need for windows affects the design.

and overhangs added, and all are constructed so that any part can be considered the front or the back.

With these "Big Box Buildings," children are also able to investigate what part light plays in architecture. No matter how the planes are arranged, the structure should provide for the illumination of its interior space. Openings such as windows and skylights have to be incorporated in the design as sources for light. Cardboard can be scored and folded to make shutters that allow partial light to enter when open and, when closed, give privacy and darkness to the interior.

As students become aware of how they experience space and how space is shaped, they can expand their explorations to include the use and organization of space on a larger scale. Although the flat floor and the stationary walls of the existing classroom restrict the kind of space available, it might be interesting to discover how many ways students can find to group their desks and arrange the classroom furniture. Such groupings call for more thought than placing one structure in an isolated environment.

Contemporary designers agree it is no longer enough to be concerned about the way a building looks; the way it relates to its environment is equally important. Building complexes like Lincoln Center and the United Nations in New York City help demonstrate the importance of the empty spaces that exist around the structures.

To introduce students to city planning, small boxes and containers representing many structures can be arranged by them to form pleasing patterns on square or rectangular bases. A ribbon work of paths and roads might serve to unify the planned community and provide avenues for transportation. Imaginary solutions for creating living spaces on varied levels should not be overlooked and might be constructed as three-dimensional models. Further research into the works of Buckminster Fuller and Paolo Soleri, two designers already concerned with housing difficulties created by increased populations and a growing scarcity of land, will provide inspiration in designing for the future.

Part II: Structure

COLUMNS

The characteristics of the column are dramatized by having children pretend to be columns. Standing erect, each student represents a vertical structure perpendicular to the ground and capable of supporting the weight of some sort of roof above the ground. The caryatids from the south porch of the Erechtheon of the Acropolis at Athens provide a classic example of columns resembling human forms and used as supports in a post-and-beam construction.

In making architectural discoveries, children need to be confronted with situations that cause them to experience structures as well as space. A tour of buildings in the neighborhood will give children a chance to stand under a porch and observe how the columns hold up the roof, or to put their arms around columns and notice the varied diameters. The shape as well as the width of columns can vary, as different materials and situations will demonstrate.

(Photograph by the author.)

A picture of a Greek temple illustrates
how columns resembling human forms
support a roof. Children then pretend
to be columns themselves and discover how many of them it takes to
hold up a roof.

Long, thin tubes of cardboard are made to stand as columns by setting them in sand and plaster of paris.

In the classroom, a thin, unstable cardboard tube taller than the child can be made to stand by inserting it into a container filled with a layer of sand and a top covering of plaster of paris. A variety of long, linear forms should provide the basis for varied and ever-changing results. Columns of corrugated cardboard made to stand by themselves are additional examples. Folded or rolled paper can be used to make columns on a smaller scale. Narrow columns fashioned of wooden dowels can be pushed into sand, into blocks of styrofoam, or into wooden bases which have been drilled. Cups, cans, boxes, and wooden blocks will stand by themselves and can be stacked into columns.

Although isolating structural elements of building is useful for understanding, the value of a lesson on columns as a principle of structure is demonstrated when incorporated with the beam.

Children experience the shelter offered by a roof supported by columns; they see that the length of the column determines the height of the roof.

76

Empty cans and styrofoam cups are used as modular units which will stand by themselves and can be stacked into graceful, vertical columns.

POST-AND-BEAM

The post-and-beam, or post-and-lintel as it is sometimes called, is one of the oldest forms of construction known to man. The geometric beauty of its structure can be seen in the exposed wooden framework of a house under construction or more dramatically in the steel-grid construction of a multi-storied skyscraper before hidden by walls of brick and glass.

I find it helpful to demonstrate the character of post-and-beam construction by having children place their index fingers in the form of a "T"; by moving the top finger slightly to left or right the instability of the connection can be seen. The necessity for adding a second post to support the beam can also be seen. The relatively solid post-and-beam structure is made lighter in weight with the use of the truss.

In model-making, careful placement and balance are important as children position cardboard beams on top of columns. This is especially true if they are working with large-scale materials. The manipulatory skills developed by working with three-dimensional materials are as important to young children as the skills developed through

Wooden dowels offer an example of post-and-beam construction with thin supports, while foam blocks appear as a solid mass. Balancing a cardboard roof on one column shows that the stability of the structure is fragile until a second column is added.

the cutting and pasting exercises used in other art projects.

As students position a roof upon thin columns the start of a house with large, open spaces is suggested. The tall columns of cardboard tubes

Children discover unique model-making materials to implement the principle of post-and-beam construction. They become deeply engrossed in balancing the structural elements.

MASONRY CONSTRUCTION

Each age has used and has been concerned with the materials and technology available at the time. With the technological advances during the last century, masonry construction is no longer as important as it once was. Now that steel and concrete make preformed slab-sided buildings possible, it does not seem logical to have young children spend hours building masonry walls for models. Learning how to place bricks one at a time by using sugar cubes or small blocks of wood seems more suitable for a class in building concepts than for one devoted to concepts of designing architecture. The design principles involved in masonry walls and arches can best be investigated through the use of more direct model-making materials. Cardboard walls, for instance, can be constructed with graphic symbols for brick or stone applied by sketching or painting.

provide a good scale. Let children discover how many columns are needed to support a roof. Let them discover how many of them can find shelter under one roof. Provide comparisons in height by using columns of several lengths. Let children crawl or bend in order to fit into the spaces created. The scale of a large model helps give children some feeling of their size and position in space in relation to what they are constructing.

Experiences in tactile perception are important to understand the stacking of materials in a masonry wall. Sugar cubes are a favorite material.

Though the historical importance of masonry construction cannot be overlooked and though children are quick to react favorably to Egyptian and Aztec pyramids and to Medieval castles, copying masonry construction usually results in unimaginative, walled-in designs. The functional concepts behind such structures do provide an opportunity for more creative designs when other construction techniques and materials are introduced. (See the discussion of castles on pages 114 to 118.)

Historically, the tremendous weight of masonry walls did limit construction possibilities. The introduction of iron and steel made it possible not only to build structures higher than ever before, using the post-and-beam construction, but also to diverge from the rectangular forms of that construction when desired. The lattice framework of the Eiffel Tower is just one example of a linear skeleton differing in form from the rectangular framework of the typical skyscraper.

LINEAR SKELETONS AND SPACE FRAMES

The "A" frame house is a familiar example of a simple linear skeleton. Other letters of the alphabet also have structural qualities suitable for ar-

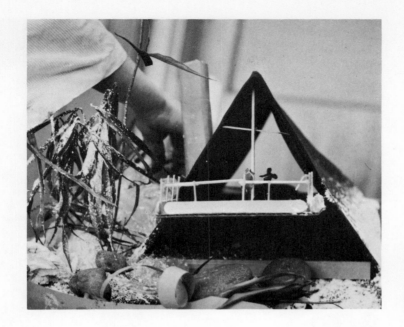

Unlike masonry construction, linear skeletons can take many different shapes. The "A" frame house is a familiar example; other letters of the alphabet also have structural qualities.

chitectural adaptations. "T" forms are found in post-and-beam construction. The "I" beam is used in constructing frameworks for skyscrapers. As an exercise for classroom exploration let every student take a different letter of the alphabet and construct a three-dimensional model based on the linear elements of that letter. Perhaps an initial from the student's own name will be inspirational. Inventive combinations and groupings made by turning the letters upside down or placing them on their sides should present possibilities for constructing linear frameworks.

Linear frameworks need not be enclosed by stationary walls. The umbrella, which provides shelter on a rainy day, and the camping tent, which provides shelter for an overnight hike, consist of lightweight structural elements which are covered with soft fabric. If children are free to experience and capture space through architectural explorations, they will undoubtedly discover architecture based on linear skeletons with soft skins (outer coverings) as a solution to their ever-changing needs.

Structural supports need not be enclosed by stationary walls and the latticelike quality of the framework can be emphasized, as in Montreal's Expo '67 Community and Man Pavilion (photograph by the author) and in these three-dimensional models.

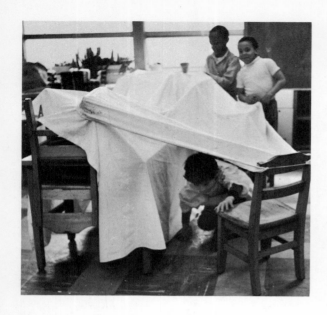

A discarded bed sheet draped over classroom furniture allows children to improvise and crawl into more expandable structures than those offered by a rigid box. At the same time, the forms created are temporary and can easily be changed. Clothespins or clamps help hold the cloth in position while the youngsters move about inside. To translate the experiences to a smaller scale, a paper napkin or a handkerchief can be draped over any three-dimensional form. Building a tepee from a half-circle of cloth also illustrates the use of structural supports. Building a tepee from paper or oak tag, however, changes the structural concept because both materials will stand by themselves and need no skeletal framework.

Discarded bed sheets become temporary shelters; the tepee is an example of soft-skin architecture employing structural elements to support a soft covering.

Further investigation of structural supports might be conducted outside (if the weather is pleasant), in the school gymnasium, or on the auditorium stage, using poles and a long bolt of material. Several bed sheets might be sewn together or an army surplus parachute might be used. The children can be asked to hold onto the corners of the cloth and by pulling it taut raise it off the ground. The poles can be used to change the height of the roof in various places.

Buckminster Fuller among others has described the strength and function of the ridge pole, which is used in this way to take advantage of the pull of gravity in relation to building. As another advocate of lightweight architecture, Frei Otto has developed exciting draped forms that are highly complex.

Space frames further emphasize the use of linear structural members. Space frames are lightweight structures that cover the maximum amount of space with the minimum number of structural elements and minimum weight. Because of its basic strength as a frame, the equilateral triangle often becomes the module. The rigidity of the triangular shape can be demonstrated by comparing it with square or rectangular frames of paper or cardboard pinned together with paper fasteners.

A temporary tent is improvised from a long bolt of cloth. Poles are used to change the height of the roof. Similarly draped forms were developed by architect Frei Otto in his design for the German Pavilion at Expo '67. (Photograph by the author.)

Lightweight space frames are constructed of a minimum number of structural elements. Equilateral triangles are combined to form tetrahedrons ranging from toothpick size to large wooden frames.

has dried, they can then be assembled into three-dimensional units.)

Some children show endless patience in relating the concept of space frames using toothpicks. Others become frustrated and build unimaginative log cabins. A group of sixth graders, after making a toothpick model, constructed an 18-foot high wooden tetrahedron large enough for a class of thirty to fit inside but light enough for three people to lift.

To make space frames, beams and trusses can be assembled from linear members, using strips of cardboard or other similar materials. Tetrahedrons and prism-shaped skeletons can be grouped in horizontal or vertical directions with additional structural members glued in place if needed for support. (The triangles and other geometrically shaped modules used to make the tetrahedrons and prisms can be formed first and, once the glue

Hollow soda straws and tightly rolled sheets of newspaper are just two kinds of material suitable for making tetrahedron space frames.

Sheets of cardboard cut into narrow strips of almost any length provide linear members with a longer scale than that offered by toothpicks, and the strips are less tedious for the young designer. Other materials with a similar proportion are plastic or bamboo reeds, coffee stirrers, tongue depressors, popsicle sticks, or soda straws. Because soda straws are hollow they can be strung together, while other materials can be pinned or glued. "Geo-D-Stix" and "Moby Lynx" are available commercially and incorporate sophisticated joining devices.

Two sheets of newspaper tightly rolled and then taped or tied together provide slightly larger units. Long cardboard tubes from bolts of fabric can be

Children form human arches to capture the rhythmic movement of arches they have seen in slides of Venice. (Photograph of Doges Palace by the author.)

drilled and then wired together to form tetrahedrons and prism-shaped skeletons.

THE ARCH

There are several ways to show the structural and decorative application of arches as a repeated movement in space. One way is to show slides and pictures of historic examples; another is to find contemporary examples during a class trip. Furthermore, children should be able to learn about this structure in space through physical

apart and with raised arms to place the palms of their hands together. In that way, they formed a structural arch. Together, they raised their arms higher, while each child pushed inward and helped stabilize the other. Standing in a straight line, a group of students repeated the same experience to form a tunnel. By standing in a circle they formed a dome. To further demonstrate the application of arches to architecture, I cut arches from large sheets of cardboard to suggest doorways and windows.

As flexible wooden shapes are bent into arches, children learn they must stoop down to fit through the diminished space.

participation. I took a class outside one day and asked the students to bend long, thin strips of wood. Two children were asked to hold onto the ends of an extremely long piece of wood and slowly, but evenly, begin to push inward. As the arch grew higher and higher, the class could see the distance between the two children diminish. As this happened, the open space created became as important as the wooden structure.

Next, I asked two children of about the same height to stand facing each other several feet

The continuity of the arch is stressed in drawing its form.

Returning to the classroom after these experiences, some children went to the blackboard and drew large, rhythmic movements, while others worked at their desks. With a handful of paper strips, some glue, and a cardboard base, arches, vaults, tunnels, and domes were combined in rhythmic ways that suggested roller coasters, amusement parks, and the fantastic architecture of a World's Fair.

The strength of the arch, like that of the spiral, was found to be in its continuity. I favor using materials that are continuous—like paper, reed, or

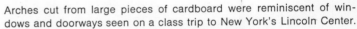

Arches cut from large pieces of cardboard were reminiscent of windows and doorways seen on a class trip to New York's Lincoln Center.

97

An arrangement of paper-strip arches creates the effect of a roller coaster at a World's Fair.

Pariscraft material is dipped in water, draped to form an inverted arch, and allowed to harden in that shape.

wire—and find that they are more appropriate for young children to use than individual, wedge-shaped units place one upon another to emulate masonry construction. Individual units are tedious to use.

Arches are combined to form a dome.

The length of the material used affects the height and span of the curve. A progression of shapes from low to high, or from narrow to wide, might be incorporated in the design. Pinching the center or other part of a paper arch changes the shape. Placing four or more arches together so that their bases form a circle changes the structure to a ribbed dome.

DOMES

A dome considered as a volume is an upside-down basket or bowl. Considered as a structure, though, it presents variations. Brunelleschi's dome (1420-1436) on the Cathedral of Florence, Italy, and the geodesic one by Buckminster Fuller at

Two different domes show how the final form can vary. Top is geodesic
dome (U.S. Pavilion, Montreal's Expo '67) by Buckminster Fuller. Bot-
tom is concrete dome (Royal Pavilion, Brighton, England) by John Nash.
(Photographs by the author.)

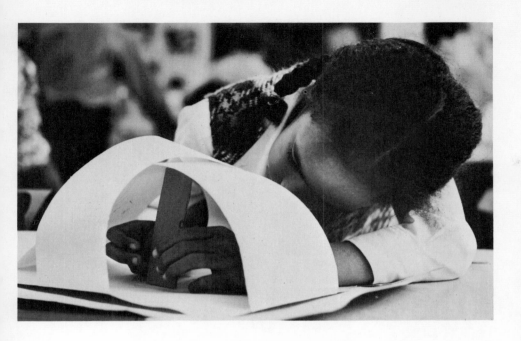

Expo '67, Montreal, Canada (United States Pavilion) offer a contrast in materials and construction, since Brunelleschi's is of masonry and Fuller's is a space-frame structure. A dome of reinforced concrete illustrates an additional contrast in structure.

Children can make domes by using papier-mâché over plastic bowls. Once the newspaper and paste have dried, the plastic bowl is removed and the papier-mâché shell is ready to be designed as part of a modern building. For imaginative buildings, several domes might be combined

Egg cartons present preformed domes that can be arranged into new structures.

with cardboard tubes, tin cans, and plastic bottles.

These papier-mâché domes can also serve as an introduction to reinforced concrete shells and other molded and poured structures, with an emphasis on similarities and differences in construction and form.

Papier-mâché domes serve as an excellent introduction to molded and poured shell structures.

MOLDED AND POURED STRUCTURES

The exterior form of a reinforced concrete shell conceals a continuous, interlocking, interior skeleton comparable in pattern to an intricate weaving and much different in construction from the ribbed dome or from the post-and-beam. These intricately designed grids make it possible to build sweeping curves and other freely flowing forms as well as spherical domes, something which masonry construction does not allow. The grids strengthen or reinforce the concrete, which is poured into wooden molds until it hardens into the desired forms.

While it is not necessary to construct such grids for model-making, students should get an idea of the basic strength of such a system of construction. Have each student feel the strength of the grid formed by interlocking his own fingers. To further illuminate the mystery of the interior skeletons existing in molded or poured structures but hidden from the eye, structural engineering may be related to the internal structure of the hand and the framework of the human body as these are examined through X rays.

Lincoln Center's huge band shell and a contemporary playground structure are two examples of the freely flowing forms that are possible when concrete is poured into a form. The reinforcing grids are not visible when the structure is finished.

(Courtesy of Form, Inc.)

Covering an inflated balloon with Pariscraft is an easy way to make a model of a concrete shell. Openings can be cut into the dried shell. Other forms, like jugs, can also be used as the base for a Pariscraft shell.

Students will find it easy to make a model of a concrete shell by covering a balloon with papier-mâché or with Pariscraft, which dries more quickly. When the mâché form has dried, it can be combined with other shapes and forms for architectural designs. The balloon can be deflated and openings can be cut in the mâché form to change the existing shape or to suggest doors and windows.

The principle of the inflated balloon is actually used in constructing shells and free-form structures which are made of urethane plastic. The plastic foam is sprayed onto inflated forms, which are deflated when the foam has hardened. These structures do not require the grids used with concrete.

Students might begin creating free-form models by folding pieces of paper.

Designed by Felix Drury, this house in Georgia was actually built by spraying urethane-plastic foam over inflated fabric balloons and allowing the foam to harden. (Photograph by John Zimmerman, from *American Home* Magazine.)

A long rectangle of paper and a circular paper plate permit different solutions to the exercise in space sculpture.

The student designer might begin to create free-flowing architectural forms by folding, bending, twisting, or scoring a single piece of paper in exercises suggestive of Origami. In creating these space sculptures, a variety of shapes and sizes of paper should be used in experimenting with free-flowing roofs and walls. For example, a long rectangle would permit different solutions than a square or a circular paper plate.

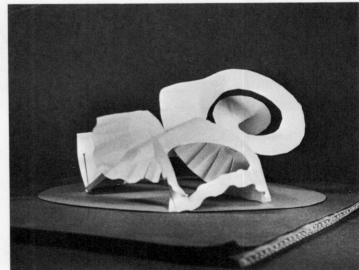

Different shells can be formed over a flexible framework consisting of a wire coat hanger and a nylon stocking. Applying newspaper and wheat paste (or Pariscraft) to the taut skin will make the form more permanent. The finished shell can then be landscaped.

Additional free-form models that suggest foamed plastic or concrete shells may be constructed from a flexible framework made with a coat hanger covered by a nylon stocking. The wire coat hanger offers structural support for the soft-skin covering of the stocking, which is pulled over the hanger and tied closed. Once the open end of the stocking has been tied, the wire can be pulled into a sculptural shape that will cause the stocking to stretch and form a taut skin. Applying newspaper strips dipped in wheat paste will make the soft skin more permanent. When dry, the hard covering can be painted. Sand and grass can be used to landscape the form built to resemble a seaside sunshade or housing shell.

An air-conditioner filter, or some chicken wire, also makes a good framework for a shell. Drawing reflects the simple shape of a shell model.

An architectural shell can also be formed by cutting a used air-conditioner filter out of its frame. Chicken wire or window screening is similar in potential. Because the metal is more difficult to shape than the hanger-and-stocking frame, models should be kept simple and direct in concept. The task is made easier if rectangular strips and geometric shapes are cut from the large shape before it is distributed to the students. Once formed, shapes can be grouped and covered with papier-mâché.

113

Appreciation of architecture can begin in the neighborhood.

Part III: Appreciation

Appreciation of architecture can begin in the neighborhood. Every community has its own architecture and young children cannot help being influenced by what they see. Unfortunately, much that they see is mediocre, but many good examples can be found.

I see no need to present any listing of great buildings or great architects for children to memorize. Although studying what others have done is important, students should be encouraged to think for themselves in evaluating past accomplishments as well as in designing new forms. A vari-

ety of experiences and motivations during the art period should stimulate individuals to make their own critical selections, based upon personal research, judgment, and investigation. An important objective should be to disclose the variety and uniqueness of architectural examples. The dynamics of structure and space should introduce architecture as organic and ever-changing.

Relating structures of the past to their time and place in history helps to develop the view that architecture is responsive to changing needs. An investigation of castles from the Medieval and

Renaissance periods, for example, provides an opportunity to deepen awareness of architectural details and to further interest in the historical reasons behind these details.

As a teacher, you might take specific historical conditions of the Middle Ages and phrase them as a hypothetical problem for the students to solve. Experiment by telling the students: "Imagine you are living at a time in history when there are pirates and raiders. You are very wealthy; you have all the money you want and access to building any kind of fortification that you can in order to protect yourself and your family and friends from enemies.

Historical examples introduce far-ranging investigations. Students can, for instance, construct their own versions of a castle from various materials. Cardboard provides strong walls, while sand results in an organic structure.

"In designing your home, consider the location you would select to give maximum security. Would you build it on a mountain or a hilltop? Would you float it over a body of water, surround it with a moat, or submerge it under the water's surface? Would you build your house into the ground, or position it off the ground, or even locate it underground?"

The students can try to answer these questions by constructing their own versions of a castle or fortified shelter. Investigation of the parts of a castle as well as its overall function can be developed as models are made. A balance of direction and suggestion from the teacher will act as a catalyst to the imagination. Children can be called upon to suggest and collect possible art materials needed to represent walls which would be strong. Egg cartons, cardboard, tubes, cans, boxes, and wood are all useful. In the classes I taught, sand provided the most organic and spontaneous castle designs.

The children in my classes attacked the problem enthusiastically. Some stacked materials to represent masonry walls. Then they designed battlements and placed them on the tops of the walls for added defense purposes. Towers were added

for purposes of observation. Children seemed to love the movement that drawbridges offered in opening and closing. With a large-scale model constructed from cardboard boxes, the children had the experience of raising and lowering a cardboard drawbridge to the floor and actually walking inside their castle.

Children may not realize that castles exist today because they associate them with fairy tales and

Drawbridges, observation towers, and other parts of a castle were stressed in terms of serving a function.

stories of knights in shining armor. Books, magazines, and postcards are available which offer pictures for reference and motivation. Paintings from the Renaissance are an excellent reference source because artists of that period often included castles as part of the landscape in their paintings. Examining pictures and model-making experiences are both part of a back-and-forth process involved in learning. The results of the model-making may be as straightforward or imaginative as children and teachers wish. The variety and scope of the class activities give added dimension to the total educational impact.

Everyday art ideas and seasonal themes can provide the means for a more unusual approach to appreciating architecture. At Halloween, shadow puppets of ghosts and witches and cut-out silhouettes of a "haunted house" open the door for a discovery of Victorian houses with "gingerbread" motifs. Using silhouettes of Victorian houses as props for the action of shadow puppets, eerie attics, or porches with ornately carved railings, or highly embellished walls become focal areas for study.

Children can also relate one architectural experience to another. A class of second graders who had been studying Thomas Jefferson's Monticello as an example of farm communities and "Houses with a History" were intrigued to learn that Andrea Palladio had designed some very similar "villas" in Italy several hundred years before Jefferson

At Halloween, haunted-house shadow puppets provide an opportunity to introduce Victorian architecture.

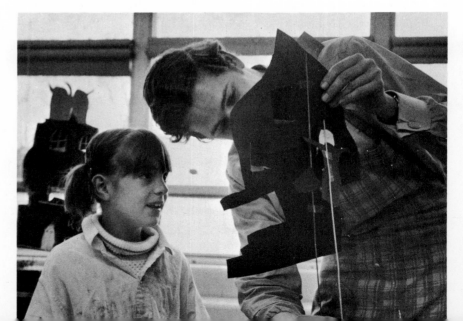

designed Monticello. They were also interested in seeing how Jefferson's design in turn influenced the architecture of Southern plantations. As they continued their study, the shape and function of farm buildings such as barns became an important part of their knowledge. These forms projected in a landscape with a background and foreground helped in developing their sense of perspective and composition.

In stimulating an appreciation of architecture, examples of past accomplishments should serve as a point of departure for contemporary architecture and not as hard facts to be copied. A model or a picture of a Greek temple may motivate an investigation of post-and-beam construction and the influence of the classic style on present-day tastes, but to reconstruct a model of the Parthenon should not be the purpose of the lesson in design. The forms children create do not have to resemble what they have seen. Their curiosity should be further aroused by constantly exposing them to modern architectural situations in which current methods and materials are used.

A study of both the old and the new develops an appreciation of architecture as an ever-changing art. The Parthenon in Athens, Greece, provides a contrast with a modern house in Split, Yugoslavia. (Photographs by the author.)

Trips outside the classroom offer invaluable experiences. These class members sketched what they saw at the Guggenheim Museum, which was designed by famous architect Frank Lloyd Wright.

4
TRIPS

Trips are an invaluable source of inspiration and relate classroom experiences to the real world. A walking trip around the neighborhood or a trip in a bus to another neighborhood or another city creates a classroom without walls.

In order to make a trip more than just a visual experience, children should be called upon to participate. By putting their arms around columns, they will find that these structures vary in size and shape. In some instances it will be possible to find the distance around the trunk of a large tree only

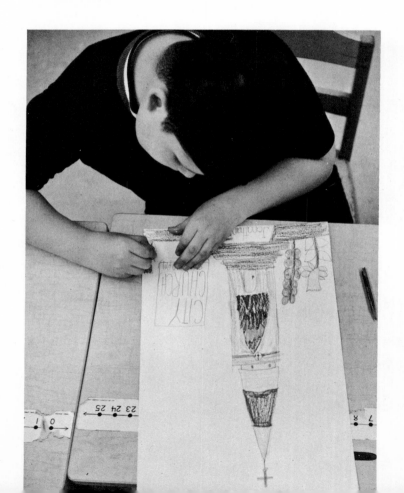

(Left) Children are asked to participate in making discoveries, such as finding the thickness of a porch column.

Drawings revealed that each trip increased the student's powers of observation.

if several children hold hands. Standing under a porch seems a natural and appropriate place to discover that columns are perpendicular to the base and usually offer support for an overhead covering.

Children can feel texture by running their fingers over the cracks of a brick wall. A crayon rubbing might be made to show the surface quality of a masonry wall and of other materials and pat-

After a visit to an historic building (right), students drew a class mural of the details they saw along the way.

terns found along the way. By pointing out what occurs as they walk up steps, a perceptive teacher can make children aware that direction and position in space are important. Calling their attention to questions—like "How many steps are there?" and "Which hand do you use to hold the railing?" —helps bring greater detail into the pictures children do when they return to the classroom.

A casual observation may not reveal the well-planned nature of a trip. One trip I organized was based on a scavenger hunt in which the hiding place for each clue had been selected to point out an architectural detail. Everyone was excited by the idea of a hunt. Four teams, each chaperoned by a "classroom mother" or a teacher, were to set out separately, with each team in search of a separate picture puzzle hidden in envelopes along its route. Having separate teams would eliminate the confusion of a long line of children walking together. If each group went in a different direction, the sidewalk would not be crowded and the children would have more opportunity to talk and make discoveries as they walked.

Maps of the community had previously been made and studied. Directions for the hunt were given. Each envelope along the route contained a piece of the picture puzzle and a written clue to the location of the next piece of the puzzle. Finding each envelope was essential in locating the next puzzle piece and clue. Each hiding place focused on some aspect of architecture, such as a window ledge or a porch railing. When all the pieces of the puzzle were found, they would become a picture of a well-known building. An envelope containing a map giving the locations of all the clues was given to each team leader and was to be opened only if the group became lost or could not find a clue. To start, every team had one clue located in the school. The last clue gave the direction to return to the classroom and begin drawing a picture that would show *where* the picture puzzle pieces had been located.

The first team back helped distribute paper to everyone and as the others came in the chatter was, "Sarah, we saw your mother . . . Jonathan, we talked to your uncle at the firehouse . . . We went past your house, Helen." Some children started putting together their puzzle pieces. One completed puzzle showed the "Singer Building" by John Marin; the others were "Manchester Valley" by Joseph Pickett, a scene of Montmartre by Utrillo, and a photograph of the Lever House.

As the children began drawing, I could see that the boy who had found a clue under a porch railing had gained a new understanding of the structure of a railing. The child who had knocked on the front door of her house to find her mother presenting her with an envelope showed a greater sense of detail in her drawing. The child who had found a clue taped to the flagpole showed that the pole next to the one-storied school was tall.

As some children finished the assignment, they began cutting their own drawings apart to make their own picture puzzles. Most important, though, they had become aware of architectural details seen along their route and had gained a knowledge of the route itself.

Awareness of the directions taken on a walking trip gives children a way of orienting themselves and is especially important if a classroom mural is to be made later. The children should be able to answer such questions as: "Can you show how you turned to the right and then to the left? Where did you cross the street? Were there any streets you saw along the way but did not cross? Can you show the brick house with the porch, the wooden house with the shutters, or the house with columns? Can you show the houses with the steps in front? What else did you see?"

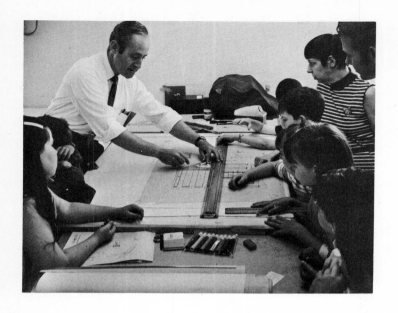

As part of the study of how buildings are designed, a trip to an architect's office might be arranged, or an architect might be asked to visit the classroom to explain the nature of his work and the special training and equipment it requires. Floor plans, renderings, and models are visual examples which generally impress children.

Children learn about materials, floor plans and renderings during a visit to an architect's office.

A list of quickly moving questions seems to bring a multitude of answers as the children draw their observations. They can work individually at their desks or directly on the mural, using a long roll of paper stretched across the blackboard for the latter. One child can be asked to draw the path on the mural, while the other students make crayon pictures or paintings on separate sheets of paper at their desks. The pictures can be cut out and then arranged and pasted on the mural as a group project and record of the trip taken.

ings. A follow-up after the building is completed presents a comparison for study.

If trips are taken which encompass totally new situations for most children, mimeographed trip guides might be prepared and taken along. The guides should have large, empty spaces on the paper for children to sketch in their observations stimulated by key words or questions printed on the paper. This kind of direction provides motivation and incentive for making the trip a personal discovery.

A trip to the construction site of a new building is a fascinating experience for children. If ceilings are unfinished and pipes and wiring are exposed, if bulldozers and cranes are still to be seen, the students will exploit these details in their draw-

A sketching trip to a construction site provokes a deep interest in the elaborate steel structure.

Observation offers clues to how children work.

The teacher should assist students in learning objectives that will later be tested, such as getting materials to stay together.

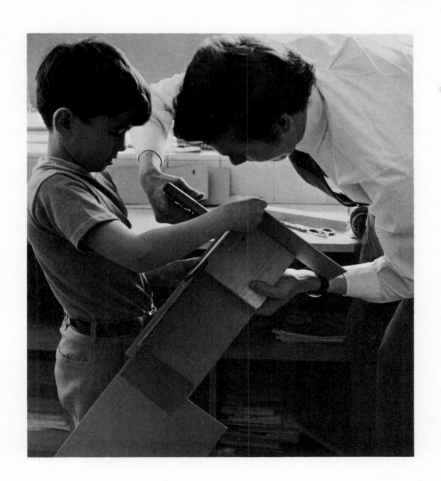

5

EVALUATION

As an integral part of the art experience, the teacher's evaluation of a student's performance can be helpful if the teacher uses criteria based on intelligence and "cognitive openness." On the other hand, too many rules and regulations can hinder and obstruct creative designing.

Although an architectural work can only be evaluated as a total statement in relationship to its environment, the principles and concepts involved can be isolated for understanding and analysis. In attempting to derive criteria from this analysis, the teacher must remember that one concept cannot help but overlap another.

In formulating each lesson or series of lessons, an initial plan is valuable. What is to be tested or measured should be identified before a lesson begins. These objectives may then serve as an indication of teaching effectiveness. This initial guide should allow the teacher to be prepared to accept the expected as well as to appreciate the unexpected.

Testing for names and dates seems easiest to evaluate but can be extremely limiting and of little value in the art program. The art period should not become cluttered with pencil-and-paper tests but should evoke a more ambitious atmosphere for learning.

The most important things happen as children work with space and materials. The following is an example of a behavioral objective in the area of art studio performance; in this case the student is called upon to use both the concept of creating vertical movement and the principle of slotting things together.

Given 3-inch plastic squares, and rectangles, circles, and open-ended cylinders of a similar size—all slotted so they can fit together—the first-grade student should be able to construct a vertical structure at least 18 inches tall, and will then be able to make a picture of his structure. The fact that this task sounds elementary does very little to designate the appearance of the finished product. It allows the student to select the shapes he

A sketch is not expected to be a photographic reproduction but rather a balance of drawing skill and creative interpretation.

desires and put them together the way he wishes. It requires the student to understand the meaning of vertical and tests his ability to get things to stay together. It also measures his ability to translate his three-dimensional project into a graphic interpretation.

The same objective could be rewritten to present the problem of building a horizontal construction with the same materials. Additional limitations could be defined if desired (e.g., the amount of time allowed for the task; the size of the base supplied to the student; the number of pieces used, with fewer pieces requiring a greater efficiency in construction; and/or an increase in the height).

Behavioral objectives can be specified in terms of how you expect the student to perform; these objectives should give direction in planning lessons and in making evaluation possible. They should be applicable and appropriate for the particular individual or group of individuals involved. As the students' training grows more extensive, objectives may become more specific or "open-ended" as desired. They can be changed and redefined as projects are redirected for added dimension or emphasis. As I have mentioned, it

Children's drawings show varied degrees of maturity.
Drawings may be made from memory or from models.

seems apparent that some projects can and should be approached more than once during the elementary school years.

Special care should be given in encouraging the inventive, creative solution, although it may be more difficult to understand visually than the unimaginative, neatly done, pretty picture of an ordinary house with flowers. A drawing is not expected to be a photographic copy. As children grow older, though, they often feel their drawings should reflect the same images as a camera. In recognition of this, architectural renderings should be studied in terms of being neither right nor wrong, good nor bad, but instead a revelation of a variety of techniques that balance drawing skills with creative interpretation.

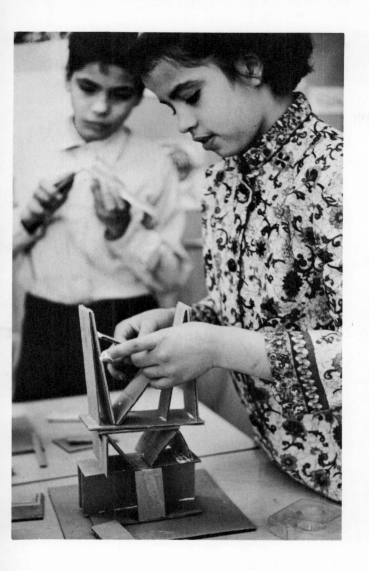

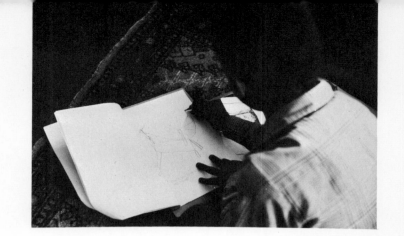

Encouraging children to talk about their work helps the teacher find out what they have set out to accomplish and makes it easier to evaluate the work.

In evaluating two-dimensional work, "checklists" of items and concepts that have been studied and therefore might be included in drawings can be useful. Although there are no "right" or "wrong" answers, the art work of some children seems to show more awareness in regard to shape, detail, the organization of the page, and the manipulation of materials than the work of other children. This seems to be reflective to some extent of a student's maturity and perception level.

If ears are prepared to listen, children can be encouraged to talk about their work. Such communication gives insight into the work and helps the teacher to evaluate it. Thoughts children offer about their work can be verbal or can be written down. Having their comments in written form helps the children carry home their experiences and gives them an even greater feeling of achievement. Short stories children usually like to tell about their pictures give the teacher evidence of their architectural terminology and vocabulary.

Observing the way children work with art ma-

How well children learn can be judged partly by watching their work habits.

terials also offers clues to their learning. Where and how children go about building can both be studied.

Do they build vertically or horizontally?

Do they design symmetrically or asymmetrically?

Do they close up all the spaces or leave open spaces?

Do they repeat certain motifs or rhythms?

Do they work alone or do they work with others?

Do they experiment or do they copy what others are doing?

The answers to these observations may tell more about the personal adjustment of children than it will about the aesthetic nature of their work. In doing so it may aid the sensitive teacher in helping children.

A method of evaluating a student's comprehension can be based on pictorial identification. This involves a picture-matching game. Twenty photographs showing different kinds of buildings would be given to the student. He would be asked to sort them into two categories. One category would show one particular kind of building in terms of function while the other would show buildings that are functionally different.

A picture-matching game tests a child's ability to make spatial relationships. Two different views of a building, such as Monticello, are shown for the child to point out similarities.

(Photographs by the author.)

The same concept might be applied to sorting the work of a particular architect or the styles of architecture. Children might also be asked to arrange pictures showing buildings from oldest to newest. A similar identification might involve sorting or labeling pictures according to building materials used, or matching a card with the name of the material written on it to the actual material. Brick, sand, stone, cement, wood, steel, or combinations of materials are all possible categories.

A visual perception test that involves making spatial relationships would call for matching two different photographs of the same building, each taken from a different viewpoint or under far different lighting conditions. Ten pictures showing the exteriors of five houses can be placed randomly on the chalk tray, where they could all be seen by the child taking the test. (Each child would take the test separately.) The tester would hand the student a trial set of two pictures showing two views of the same house and would say, "Why would you pair these two pictures as showing the same house?" For each reason given, the child would be asked to point to the object he sees as the same in both pictures. When as many of the objects were pointed to as the child was able to see by himself, he would proceed to take the test itself.

Matching interiors to exteriors is another picture game that tests perception.

The following directions would be given: "Look carefully at all these pictures. Select and group in pairs any of these pictures that you think show the same house. Do this all by yourself. You may pick the pictures up if you wish and move them around. When you have matched a pair, hand it to me."

When the child has finished, the tester will ask: "Why did you match these two? What do you see that is the same?" The child will then be expected to point to the same things in both pictures in the same way as he did in the trial set and to tell why he thinks the objects he points to are similar. Verbal responses can be recorded on a prepared sheet with a score of 1 point for each pair correctly matched, and an additional 1 point for each reason given correctly. Incorrect matches would be recorded as minus 1.

The pictures used could be collected from magazines and selected in both color and black and white. Pictures of interiors could be used for a similar test. Two pictures of the same room taken from two viewpoints would require the child to make space relationships for a correct match. Another test would match interiors to exteriors. Grouping the exterior, interior, and floor plan of the same house would be an additional possibility for picture games.

A co-operative architect offers helpful comments on a youngster's work.

A comprehensive assessment of this art program would ultimately require a time-consuming battery of tests in order to evaluate long-range, as well as immediate, goals in terms of teaching architectural history, criticism, visual perception, and art studio production. Neither time nor facilities are available in school systems to make this possible at this time. Mobile populations further complicate the task of determining the progress a child makes from one year to another.

However, the ideas and techniques discussed in this book have been used successfully and it is hoped they will be expanded even further as those who read about the program are motivated to initiate their own projects in a continuing exploration of architecture.

The projects and materials may be simple; the objectives and solutions should be varied and visually exciting. As you, yourself, become more aware and more experienced, you should become more critical and demanding of structure and space, and use this new knowledge to formulate objectives. Giving children freedom to experiment and to discover things for themselves is equally important.

The materials and projects should work together in motivating the children. Opportunities should be provided not only for the student who is interested in architectural history but also for the student who is interested in making architectural predictions for the future. The experiences provided should help all children develop an ability to manipulate art materials and become more visually perceptive as they create. Using appropriate strategies and evaluations, you can make architecture a dynamic and integrated aspect of the total art curriculum. Your efforts as a teacher, parent or interested adult are extremely important and cannot be underestimated if children are to develop a positive attitude toward architecture and the environment. With this positive impression comes an aesthetic education that is meaningful.

BIBLIOGRAPHY

Copplestone, Trewin. *Learning with Colour Architecture: The Great Art of Building.* New York: Paul Hamlyn, 1969.

Feininger, Andreas. *Form in Nature and Life.* London: Thames and Hudson, 1966. Published as *Forms of Nature and Life.* New York: Studio/Viking, 1966.

Giedion, Sigfried. *Space, Time and Architecture:* The Growth of a New Tradition. Cambridge: Harvard University Press, 1956. (5th rev. ed., 1967.)

Heyer, Paul. *Architects on Architecture: New Directions in America.* New York: Walker & Company, 1966.

Hitchcock, Henry Russell, and Johnson, Philip. *The International Style.* New York: W. W. Norton & Co., 1932; paperback, 1966.

Joedicke, Jürgen. *Architecture Since 1945: Sources and Directions.* New York: Frederick A. Praeger, 1969.

Jones, Cranston. *Architecture Today and Tomorrow.* New York: McGraw-Hill Book Company, 1961.

Ragon, Michel. *The Aesthetics of Contemporary Architecture.* Tr. by Haakon Chevalier. Switzerland: Editions du Griffon, 1968. New York: George Wittenborn, 1969.

Rasmussen, Steen Eiler. *Experiencing Architecture.* Cambridge: The M.I.T. Press, 1962.

Rudofsky, Bernard. *Architecture without Architects.* Garden City, New York: Doubleday & Company, Inc., 1964, 1969.

Wilson, Forrest. *Architecture: A Book of Projects for Young Adults.* New York: Van Nostrand Reinhold Company, 1968.

————. *Architecture and Interior Environment: A Book of Projects for Young Adults.* New York: Van Nostrand Reinhold Company, 1971.

————. *What It Feels Like to Be a Building.* New York: Doubleday & Company, Inc., 1969.

Wright, Frank Lloyd. *The Natural House.* New York: Horizon Press, 1954.

SUPPLEMENTARY MATERIALS

MANIPULATIVE TOOLS AND CONCEPT BUILDERS

BY CHILDCRAFT:
  Architectural Cards $3.00
  Balancing Benches $2.50
  Charles Eames' Deluxe House of Cards $3.00
  Childcraft Climbing House $185.00
  Childcraft play-panels $4.95
  Clink-A-Links $4.00
  Connector $12.00
  Cu-Briks $3.95
  Futura Construction Set $3.60
  Geo-D-Stix $4.95
  Hexupon $8.00
  Join-Ems. $3.95
  Ji-Gan-Tiks $2.95
  Playdome $29.95
  Playplax Rings $6.00
  Playplax Squares $3.50
  Prismatic Blocks $8.00
  Rick Rack Blocks $8.00
  See Through Nesting Blocks $7.50
  Space Panels $6.00
  Top Towers $3.00

BY CREATIVE PLAYTHINGS:
  Fantasy town $1100.00
  Flexagons $5.95
  Geo-D-Stix $4.95
  Giant foam blocks $6.50
  Tinkertoy $3.50

BY CUISENAIRE:
    Moby Lynx Construction Kits $3.95

BY FORM INC.:
    Moon House
    Playwall
    The Castle

BY MONSANTO:
    Konnecto Blocks $60.00
    Lock 'N' Stack Blocks $75.00
    Snap Wall $92.00
    Versa-Flex Blocks $24.00

BY PRESSMAN TOY CORPORATION:
    Crystal Climbers in the cylinders
    Crystal Climbers in the round
    Crystal Climbers in the square
    (all of the above called Playplax by Childcraft)

FILMS AND FILMSTRIPS

FROM EYE GATE HOUSE, INC.:

The Story of Building a House
(nine filmstrips and teacher's manual)
    How It Started
    Excavating the Cellar
    Building the Foundation
    Building the Frame of the House
    Gas, Electric, Plumbing and Other Installations
    Further Installations
    Completing the Outside of the House
    Completing the Inside of the House
    The House Is Built

The Story of Houses
(nine filmstrips and teacher's manual)
    The First Homes
    Strange Homes
    More Strange Houses
    The First Permanent Houses
    Dwellers in Tents
    Castle and Manor Houses
    Homes Around the World
    Home of the American Indians
    Homes of the United States — Old and New

FROM CHURCHILL FILMS:
The Changing City (1966)

FROM AMERICAN INSTITUTE OF ARCHITECTS:
No Time for Ugliness

FROM STERLING FILMS:
The City, Heaven and Hell
(Based on Lewis Mumford's book *The City in History*.)

FROM INTERNATIONAL FILM BUREAU:
A Is for Architecture
Brasilia
Suburban Living
Town Planning

SLIDES

FROM SANDAK, INC.:
    Complete listing of European and American Architecture

FROM SOCIETY OF VISUAL EDUCATION:
    Ancient Architecture
    Classical Architecture — Greek
    Ancient Architecture — Roman
    Renaissance Architecture
    Medieval Architecture
    American Architecture — Early
    American Architecture — Modern

COMMERCIAL RESOURCES

Acorn Structures, Inc.
Box 540
Concord, Mass. 01742

Bemiss-Jason Corporation
3250 Ash Street
Palo Alto, Calif. 94306

Bourges Color Corporation
80 Fifth Avenue
New York, N.Y. 10011
(Cutocolor, Cutotapes)

California Redwood Assn.
617 Montgomery Street
San Francisco, Calif. 94111

Childcraft
P.O. Box 280
Madison Square Station
New York, N.Y. 10010

Churchill Films
662 N. Robertson Boulevard
Los Angeles, Calif. 90069

Cotton-Barton, Inc.
2604 Sisson Street
Baltimore, Md. 21211

Creative Playthings
Princeton, N.J. 08540

Cuisenaire
12 Church Street
New Rochelle, N.Y. 10805

Deck House, Inc.
930 Main Street
Dept. NY2-9
Acton, Mass. 01720

Eye Gate House, Inc.
146-01 Archer Avenue
Jamaica, N.Y. 11435

Form Incorporated
12900 W. Ten Mile Road
South Lyon, Mich. 48178

Futuro Corporation
1900 Rittenhouse Square
Philadelphia, Pa. 19103

International Film Bureau
332 South Michigan Avenue
Chicago, Ill. 60604

Monsanto Company
800 N. Lindbergh Boulevard
St. Louis, Mo. 63166

Nationwide Adhesive Products
19600 St. Clair Avenue
Cleveland, Ohio 44117
(Mylar, Plastic-Seal)

Pressman Toy Corp.
200 Fifth Avenue
New York, N.Y. 10010

Sandak, Inc.
4 East 48 Street
New York, N.Y. 10017

Shorewood Reproductions, Inc.
724 Fifth Avenue
New York, N.Y. 10019

Society of Visual Education
1345 Diversey Parkway
Chicago, Ill. 60614

Techbuilt
127 Mount Auburn Street
Dept. T216
Cambridge, Mass. 02138

Tri-Wall Containers, Inc.
1 Dupont Street
Plainview, N.Y. 11803

U.S. Plywood
777 Third Avenue
New York, N.Y. 10017

PICTURE AND CLIPPING FILE

Apartment buildings
Arch
Architects
Ash Lawn

Barn
Bathroom
Bedroom

Castles
Châteaus
Columns
City: Chicago
City planning

Domes
Door

Egyptian architecture
Environment
Exterior